Isabel George is a writer, journalist and PR, who has worked with animal charities, and particularly the PDSA, for many years. She has previously written for children and has also worked with the Imperial War Museum on various events and exhibitions connected with the Animals at War theme.

Also by Isabel George:

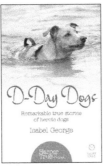
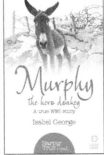

The 9/11 Dogs
The heroes who searched for survivors at the Twin Towers
Isabel George

D-Day Dogs
Remarkable true stories of heroic dogs
Isabel George

Murphy
the hero donkey
A true WWI story
Isabel George

Warrior

Warrior

The true story of
a real war horse

Isabel George

Harper
True Friend

HarperTrueFriend
An imprint of HarperCollins*Publishers*
1 London Bridge Street
London SE1 9GF

www.harpertrue.com
www.harpercollins.co.uk

First published by HarperTrueFriend 2014

© Isabel George 2014

Isabel George asserts the moral right to
be identified as the author of this work

A catalogue record of this book is
available from the British Library

PB ISBN: 978-0-00-810504-4
EB ISBN: 978-0-00-758438-3

Warrior saw action on all the major
battlefields of the Western Front during
the First World War

They said he was 'the horse the
Germans couldn't kill'

His owner recommended him for
the Victoria Cross

He was one man's best friend

A saviour of men

Warrior

'Warrior, the time has come to live up to your name. We are needed over the water in France, but don't worry; we will face this war together. We will go there, do what needs to be done and return home, please God, unscathed. So what do you say, my Warrior? What do you say?'

General Jack Seely spoke softly to his beloved horse who leant in to rest his warm cheek against his master's. Seely knew what Warrior's answer would be. The horse was made of the same fibres as his owner: nothing scared him. Already a war hero having seen conflict in the Boer War, Seely had carved a name for himself as an able horseman. Galloping across the South African veldt, he had tested the spirit of man and horse against an unforgiving environment and a merciless enemy – and won. 'Galloper Jack', as he was affectionately known, was ready to take up arms for his country once more.

It was August 1914 and Britain was at war with Germany. Seely was preparing to join a troop ship to the Western Front and this time his adventure would include his horse, Warrior, an unusually short-legged, 15.2 hands bay thoroughbred with a bright white star on his forehead. A horse whose iron will and brave heart would protect one man and inspire a nation.

Bonded forever

Warrior was born in the spring of 1908 and raised on the family estate on the Isle of Wight, where he enjoyed all the love and privilege any horse could ever need for a healthy and happy start in life. Seely was working at the Colonial Office in London when he received a telegram announcing the new arrival: *'Fine child for Cinderella born at Yafford this morning. Both doing well.'* Seely was overjoyed and excitedly shared the news with colleagues, although not all of them understood why the birth of a foal warranted the sending of a telegram. To Seely, this was family news; he was pleased to hear that the foal had delivered safely and relieved that his beloved charger, Cinderella, was doing well after the birth.

The fields of the Mottistone Downs that pitched and dipped their way to the sea were Warrior's playground. Feeling at home there, and seldom more than a few feet away from his mother, he grew into a calm and affectionate youngster. As he galloped and frolicked across the rolling countryside, Warrior also began to show that he was every bit his father's son. His sire – a handsome chestnut stallion called Straybit – had speed in his bloodline. His ancestors included horses such as Voltigeur, who won the Derby and the St Leger in 1850. The year after Warrior was born, Straybit romped home to win the Isle of Wight Lightweight race, leaving his competitors tasting the earth he kicked up in his wake.

So Warrior developed into a reflection of all that was good in his parents' characters, but there was something inside Warrior that shone beyond the good looks, gentle nature and his speed, which his master soon discovered. When Seely first rode Warrior, it was unfortunate that he chose entirely different clothes to those he had been wearing when he'd made his many visits to Cinderella and her son in the fields. Taking one look at the new outfit, Warrior wasn't sure if he wanted this man on his back! He pulled his ears back, snorted and pawed the air with his front legs. After the third time of being pitched onto the ground, Seely decided to have a quiet word with his horse and explain that they could carry on like this forever, but he would really rather they became friends. He even suggested they might be 'friends together for all our lives'. Warrior, comforted by Seely's gentle tones, dipped his head and rubbed his warm, dewy nose against his master's cheek. From that moment the two were inseparable.

Warrior

There were moments at home on the Isle of Wight, as Seely rode his young horse over the chalky Downs to the water's edge, when Warrior showed his master that he had a gift for harnessing and for denying fear its power. At first Warrior wasn't sure if he liked the sea and certainly not the breaking water, but his master encouraged him closer to the point where he could feel it ripple over his feet. He liked it. He didn't allow it to frighten him. Little by little, with patience and understanding on his side, Seely was eventually able to walk his horse into the waves. There and then he realised the courage of this horse. He might have been trembling a little at first, but then Warrior absorbed his own fear. It was Warrior's steadfast bravery as he faced the wall of tumbling water that made Seely realise his horse was not only fearless, but even radiated a sense of calm.

As a veteran of the Boer War, General Jack Seely had seen horses suffer in the most horrific ways and would not have wanted any of that for Warrior. Everyone was talking about signing up for King and Country and being home for Christmas, but Seely had devoted his civilian life to politics and he sincerely doubted the Great War would be over in four months. Even before he had returned from the war in South Africa he had been voted in as MP for the Isle of Wight, and alongside his great friend Winston Churchill (a war correspondent in the Boer conflict) he had nurtured a parliamentary career. By 1913, while Churchill accepted the role of First Lord of the Admiralty, Jack Seely was in the pivotal role of Secretary of State for War.

Seely did not rush into donating Warrior for the war effort. First, he pondered his concerns and talked them over with his friends in politics who also knew of Warrior's qualities and his suitability for the task at hand. He had already made one leap of faith in his decision to train the youngster as a charger, not a racehorse. He heard from his trainer 'Young Jim' Joliffe how his young horse showed calm intelligence and that he was wise and lovable, but he also knew that he was brave and fearless. In the spirit of Empire and all that was considered good and honourable in the service of the monarch, Jack Seely signed up for war and volunteered Warrior, too.

Warrior had no idea that he would soon be wrenched from the comfort of his mother's love. He was just four years old but he was about to embark on an episode that would require him to focus every ounce of his courage and resilience on survival. All he ever was and all he ever could be would converge at that moment.

The pair took one last gallop over the Downs together. The smell of the sea clung to their hair and clods of sweet earth spat up from the fields as Warrior pounded the ground. 'My Warrior, we are about to go on an adventure and neither of us can know what it will bring. One thing is for sure: we will be together and we will care for each other until we can ride these fields again.'

Farewell to home

Warrior had hardly been away from his mother's side since the day he was born, but early on 11 August 1914 he left behind the security and tranquillity of home to start his journey to the battlefields of the Western Front. He called to his mother as he was led from the field, and as the gate closed behind him he took one last look at home. Cinderella galloped along the edge of the field, watching her son being taken from her. She followed until she ran out of field, calling to Warrior in a language only the two of them could understand. It was a mournful, empty sound and when it stopped the silence was solid.

For weeks after her son's departure, Cinderella paced Sidling Paul – the huge pasture she now had all to herself. Wandering around with her head bowed, she had no interest in anything or anyone, despite the best efforts of the Seely children to console her. She was missing Warrior and there was no doubt that he would be missing her.

When they reached Southampton docks Seely and Warrior met a scene of chaos. Men, horses, supplies and equipment were crowded together waiting to be loaded onto the troopships. One way or another, it all had to find a way to the men at the Front.

As an officer's mount Warrior would be watched very closely by the men assigned to look after the horses during the Channel crossing. The majority of the horses around him were not so lucky. Taken from farms and fields all over Britain, the majority of the horses requisitioned by the Army that summer had never been further than their own stable, field and back yard. Now they were lined up, flanks quivering, eyes wide, waiting for their turn to be led up the gangway to the deck or settled in mass makeshift stalls in the hold.

Warrior didn't need much coaxing up the gangway, but others found the experience traumatic. When panic set in with one or two horses, the others smelled fear. There were reports of some getting so agitated that they broke free of their ropes and bolted through the docks in a bid to escape. One who made it on deck with the bustling, stomping, snorting heave of horses decided to take a leap of faith, crashing the barrier and falling overboard. As the troopships pulled away from the quay, the men and the other horses could do nothing to help the horse destined to drown.

9

Isabel George

In just two weeks the British Army had requisitioned 140,000 horses from all over Britain and all had to be transported to France in overcrowded troopships as quickly as possible. The heave and swell of the water and the cramped, sweltering conditions below deck ensured a number of the horses never completed their journey. Some fell during the voyage and broke their legs, while others were claimed by the trauma. Warrior was one of the lucky ones. Later that day, on 11 August, he trotted ashore at Le Havre with Seely by his side.

As the Special Service officer of the British Expeditionary Force, Seely was attached to the Headquarters. By the time he arrived with Warrior the HQ had already moved 20 miles closer to Paris due to the German advance. Warrior had no time to acclimatise to the fear, stink and commotion of war – the white heat from a bursting shell, the violence, the noise and the smell of blood. He had to hit the ground running. Riding through the small French villages gathering and sharing information with the local people, Seely and his steed dodged the almost constant shellfire, but Warrior never shied away. On one occasion a shell hit a stable building directly ahead of them, sending a plume of fire into the sky. Later, Seely proudly told anyone who would listen how his horse had the uncanny ability to stall fear – he felt it, but did not show it.

Many other horses would have run at that point, but not Warrior.

The experience of war had been a sudden one for Warrior. He had left the green and pleasant land of home and found himself in a place torn apart by fire and explosions. Everything a horse feared was there and it was inescapable. As Seely and Warrior joined the British Expeditionary Force's advance on the Marne, their main enemy was exhaustion. In the space of just a few weeks Warrior had grown up. He was no longer a six-year-old green to the ways of life and war; he was a survivor in a place where death was strewn all around.

The swift advance of the French Army had cut off a section of the German advance and their exhausted men were surrendering on all sides. Warrior, with Seely on his back, took a path through it all and on to La Ferté-sous-Jouarre. Suddenly, Warrior and a group of other horses from the Expeditionary Force came to a halt just as a shell landed alongside them, blowing all around it into the air. Screams erupted from the stricken and bloodied, but out of the fire and mayhem stepped Warrior. As Seely gathered a group and ran ahead to the nearest village, the German machine guns rallied. All were killed except Seely. Warrior stood just a few hundred yards away.

Seely kissed Warrior on the nose. 'If you are missing home, my Warrior, you should know that I am

Isabel George

missing it, too. This hell is so far removed from our heaven at home, and I'm sorry I can't give you a better shelter than this.' Warrior did as he always did when his master spoke so softly to him; he nuzzled his cheek. There was a moment of thankfulness between the man and his horse for the fact that, by some miracle, they had survived the onslaught. Exhausted and covered in dirt and debris, Warrior took his rest. It was not for the war horse to know what would happen next, but Seely was aware that if there was any silence on the fields of Flanders that night it would be the calm before a storm. There was already talk of the hostilities building at Ypres, and few would be spared.

The fighting was desperate. The Allied forces faced overwhelming numbers and often superior artillery along the front line, and Warrior's refusal to acknowledge fear was infectious. Every fighting man from the officer at General Headquarters to the Tommy in the trenches knew that if they slackened their grip on the enemy they would fail to hold the Channel ports and ultimately England could be lost. Seely went to report on activity at the Front only to find that it was being held by the brave survivors of an Indian contingent who refused to give in to the barrage of rifle and machine-gun fire. Warrior's legs sank into the mud that had been stirred up in the wet gloom. He kept looking around warily. He had mastered his fear of fire and shells, but he still maintained a wise respect for rifle fire. He didn't shy away or bolt, but there was unease in air. When Warrior suffered a bout of internal cramp and had to be taken back to GHQ at St-Omer, Seely breathed a sigh of relief. It seemed the unease was not unfounded – the horse Seely rode to the same spot the next day came under attack and was seriously wounded.

The informal armistice of Christmas 1914 brought a kind of peace that was welcomed by both sides. Seely heard later that soldiers from the Allied and German trenches had come together to play a game of football in No Man's Land on Christmas Day. At the same time Seely had stood and looked at the hill above the town where the Expeditionary Force was stationed and thought of home. He had taken Warrior by the bridle and whispered his plan: 'See that hill? That could be the Mottistone Downs, and for today it will be all ours. Come on, let's go!' The two galloped up the hill, taking a rare chance to ride as they would have done at home.

One of Warrior's favourite games was racing the aeroplanes as they took off from the aerodrome. He wasn't fazed by the noise of a plane's engine, as perhaps he would have been in the old days. He was used to loud, strange and terrifying sounds and remained unmoved by the raw blast of the aircrafts as they reached for the sky. Racing the planes was the nearest thing to a game that he had enjoyed on these shores, and there was no rifle fire to dodge, no

shellfire to challenge his nerves and the smell of
blood was blasted from his nostrils by the clean, cold
air.

'Three cheers for old Warrior!'

As the New Year rang in, Lord Kitchener requested Seely's presence at the War Office in London. But Seely did not travel alone. In a gesture of respect for him and his war horse, Warrior was granted a pass home, too. According to Seely in his book *Warrior: The Amazing Story of a Real War Horse*, Sir John French – Commander in Chief of the British Expeditionary Forces – allowed the horse special passage and went as far as to say: 'I owe much to your young horse ... As long as I am Commander in Chief, wherever you go, he shall go.'

Warrior travelled back home to Mottistone to visit his mother, Cinderella. Seely went to the War Office where he received his orders for the next phase of the war – he was to command the Canadian Cavalry, which comprised all the men they could muster from the bravest and best of their cavalry regiments: Lord Strathcona's Horse, the Fort Garry Horse, the Royal Canadian Dragoons and the Royal Canadian Horse Artillery. Kitchener shared the news that the Allies had experienced the first chlorine gas attack of the war during the Second Battle of Ypres and reinforcements were now urgently needed in the trenches. Seely and Warrior were to join the Canadians right away while they were training on Salisbury Plain, to help prepare them for Flanders.

General Seely was well respected by the Canadians, but his horse was respected even more. Warrior was immediately given the honour of regimental mascot, and whenever he appeared the men would shout, 'Here comes Warrior!' patting his flanks and cheering as he proudly trotted by. The men loved their horses and they were proud of the fine Canadian stock they had brought with them, so perhaps more than anyone else they understood Seely's bond with Warrior. This made the general's order to his men all the harder to deliver.

In the early months of the war it was the cavalry regiments that suffered the heaviest losses. The cavalry charge seen near Mons was such a tactical disaster that it could have been the last of the war. Waves of galloping horses ridden by men lunging swords were cut down at a distance by the relentless stutter of the German machine guns. The horses made easy targets and carnage was all that was achieved. Suddenly, the cavalry – regarded as the elite of the British Army – looked out of place, a throwback from a bygone military era. Modern trench warfare, with its barbed wire and advanced artillery, had changed the face of the fighting, and that is why, in February 1915, Seely had to ask his Canadian Cavalry soldiers to go to war without their horses.

As the men boarded the troopship at Southampton, Seely escorted Warrior onboard and eased him into a corridor where there was space enough to fit in next to him for the night crossing. It was a rough passage, and Seely was pleased that he could talk Warrior through it till dawn and offer him titbits of corn to keep his spirits up. It was 6 a.m. by the time the ship docked in Boulogne and the men could gather their kitbags ready to disembark. Several looked sick and were eager to plant their feet on dry land, but it was the General and Warrior who were the first down the gangway, positioning themselves so they could greet every man as they came ashore. There was little chatter as the men readied themselves and their belongings to move on to the next stage of their journey, but suddenly a shout went out: 'Three cheers for Warrior!' His rider must have felt the horse's body rise with pride and his head lift to acknowledge the cheering of his name. It was nothing new for Jack Seely to hear his horse praised in this way. After all, Warrior was a remarkable and lovable horse, as his owner knew only too well.

There were few home comforts for Warrior on that first night. He was used to better than being tethered behind an unsheltered haystack where the odd shell dropped or long-range bullet whizzed past. But when it happened he didn't flinch. He knew what they were and stood fast and still. He enjoyed the evenings most of all, because that was when Seely rode him round the lines to meet the men and give them a chance to chat to Warrior and stroke his ears – a comfort to them as well as the horse. Any thought of nervousness was a million miles away.

Seely's priority at every stop was to find the best billet for Warrior, and so when they reached the sector of the line just south of the Ypres Salient (where the battlefield projected into enemy territory) he was delighted to discover, under Hill 63, something that looked like a proper stable. It lacked a roof but the manger and hayrack more than made up for that, and even Warrior looked proud of his new accommodation. He nodded his head – in approval, Seely assumed. It was certainly closer to what he was used to, even if the rations were not up to scratch. Nevertheless, it was a good base for the next stage of their advance, which was over a ridge screened by trees.

During the summer of 1915 Warrior enjoyed galloping over the ridge and down into the valley, managing to visit the support line unseen by the enemy. But as the summer wore on the shell blasts swept away most of the foliage, leaving the screen less secure and the horses visible, even from a distance. A salvo of shells hit the spot where the horses stood. One shell split as it hit the ground. A piece of it was blasted straight into the chest of Warrior's companion, slicing the horse in half. Warrior stood on the spot until he saw his master come into view, and then he took off at a gallop to meet him. Neighing loudly and throwing his head in the air, the horse must have wanted to reassure Seely that although the scene was horrific, he was not going to leave his master. After all, they had made a pact to be together always.

Knowing the depth of feeling between man and horse, it's perhaps no surprise that Warrior decided that if he wasn't being ridden by Seely then he was going to follow him everywhere – just so he didn't lose sight of him again. He even broke free of his stable one day to follow the General like a big dog at his heels. Maybe he felt his luck was running out, but if he did then he was to be proved wrong. Making their next camp at a farmhouse close to the front line, Seely was relieved to discover that the stable had a door so Warrior could enjoy some protection from the elements and flying artillery. But within hours the General was woken by the sound of Warrior trying to crash the door down with his fore-feet. Recognising the sound and realising who was doing it, he ran to investigate. As he pulled open the door Warrior dashed out, just ahead of a shell erupting and destroying the building. Did the horse sense it? No one could possibly know, but quite how Warrior managed to walk free without so much as a scratch was yet another miracle.

Warrior's uncanny ability to survive against the odds was something the Canadians found totally inspiring. It was no wonder they were heard to say, 'The bullet has not been made that can kill Warrior.' They loved that horse as much as their General did, and his charmed life seemed to carry a message right to their hearts: 'If Warrior can survive this mayhem then we can, too.'

The winter of mud

The war had gone underground and the trenches that had become home to the soldiers on both sides of the conflict were flooded and rat infested – hotbeds for disease. Above and beyond the trenches there was mud: mud in every direction and as far as the eye could see. In the winter of 1915 no one could escape its influence in or out of the trenches. It became a death trap for the horses desperately trying to pull the gun carriages and wagons carrying supplies and ammunition to the front line. The wagon drivers who survived the enemy shelling and the snipers lying in wait for them at 'Hell Fire Corner' (on the Menin Road, the main route in and out of Ypres) still had to face the horror of the drowning mud at the line. Crippled vehicles and dead horses lay on the shell-pitted road for all to see, and on the battlefield the bodies of the dead became one with the stinking mud. But there was worse to come.

After eight months of seeing action on foot, the Canadians under Seely's command were reunited with their horses as the cavalry was ordered to re-form. In the lead-up to the Battle of the Somme the men left the trenches and returned to the countryside, where, almost out of earshot of the shelling, they embraced the peacefulness and the horses they had been asked to leave behind. The spring and early summer of 1916 were happier times for the men, and most particularly for the horses. Jack Seely's son, Frank, came over to join his father, bringing with him his sparky little Arab pony Akbar. Warrior and Akbar became great friends over the next two and a half years and managed to get themselves into a few scrapes. It was while they were stabled in an ancient but grand chateau that Warrior developed a taste for wattle and daub and decided to eat his way out of the building. There was no need for him to eat the walls – the food was as good as it ever was at home and he was groomed and kept busy with the training schedule – so why he did it was a mystery.

Watching the horses enjoy the beach near the chateau was a delight after the horrors of Ypres. Warrior and Akbar loved the sea and when they cantered into the shallows they would often paw at the water, begging it to rise over their backs. One day Seely took a bold step and removed their saddles and bridles so they could roll in the foam at the water's edge and immerse their weary legs in the brine. The great friends played like happy toddlers in a place that appeared to be a million miles away from war.

When he wasn't enjoying his downtime, Warrior was out on manoeuvres with Seely, who was keen for his Canadian Cavalry to be at their fittest and ready to take on the challenge of the Allied masterplan and emerge victorious from the so-called 'Big Push'. All along a 25-mile stretch of the River Somme, infantry regiments from Britain and her Empire were preparing to engage with the enemy. The idea was that the infantry would break the German front line and the cavalry would then sweep through the gap and take the enemy from the rear. By the time Warrior and Seely were ready to bring the Canadians onto the Somme battlefield, nearly two million shells had been dropped on the German lines in a bid to destroy their trenches and clear the barbed wire, even before the infantry had begun their climb over the top at 7 a.m.

General Jack Seely was chosen to lead the attack by the mounted brigade and he chose Warrior to carry him into battle. On 1 July 1916, 2,000 horses and men from the Canadian Cavalry Brigade stood 1,200 yards behind the front line. Warrior, with Seely, his son Frank and his aide-de-camp Antoine, stood just 800 yards behind the front line. The horses were fit and had trained to the sound of machine-gun and rifle fire, and now they were primed to follow Warrior at a gallop through the

German lines to victory. Behind them stood a further cast of thousands from other cavalry regiments, including the Hussars, the Bengal Lancers, Dragoon Guards and Household Cavalry. With their pennants flying in the summer breeze, they readied themselves to charge the enemy. The scene was set for what was expected to be a military walkover for the Allied forces.

Warrior stood firm, although the bombardment by the battery of 18-pounder guns was intense and made the earth jolt under his feet. Lying on his front on the ground next to his horse, the General held Warrior's reins firmly in his hand. He felt Warrior shake as the first shell broke, but there was no sign of fear after that. The group waited in the shelter of a slight hollow for news of the infantry's progress. They waited and waited, with the thud and roar of the guns pounding all around them. The horses were set for the charge and many were becoming difficult to hold back.

Word came down the line: the infantry had broken through and taken two lines of trenches. 'This is it, my Warrior. Our time has come, as we knew it would. For King and Country ...' Seely spoke softly to his horse as he jumped into the saddle and signalled to his squadron to follow him at a gallop out of the valley and up the hill to embark on the follow-through as planned. Warrior thundered ahead, showered with shouts of encouragement by the advancing troops. With Frank and Antoine riding alongside him and a squadron following behind, Seely and Warrior attracted the fury of the German artillery. As they rose out of the valley a shell fell in the middle of the group, killing and maiming the horses – except Warrior, who appeared out of the heat and smoke unhurt. But then, as they reached the foot of the ridge, they made a grim and disappointing discovery. The infantry had reached an impasse and there was nowhere for the cavalry to go. Warrior's moment on that fateful day was over, and the group had no choice but to gallop back and attend to their dead and wounded. At 3 p.m. the order came down the line: the cavalry was to stand down.

Every day for weeks as the battle raged, Seely's Canadians and the rest of the cavalry were in a state of constant readiness. The pressure on the men and the horses was evident. Each morning the General rode Warrior to the front line to see what, if anything, could be done. On the one day he decided to rest Warrior and take another horse, the poor soul was hit and killed by a shell. The Germans had not been destroyed by the bombardment at all. When it had started they had taken to their deep dugouts and stayed there until the bombardment eased, giving them the opportunity to line up their machine guns to face the waves of Allied infantry coming over the top towards them. The infantry met machine guns and advanced nowhere. There was nothing for the cavalry to follow up. On the first day of the battle alone, British Army casualties numbered 60,000, with over 20,000 in the first hour. It was indeed the darkest day in British military history.

The Battle of the Somme wound to its pitiful end on 18 November 1916, but it almost came sooner for Warrior. One night, he was found writhing and lashing out in pain, throwing himself around his stable, and Seely knew that his beloved horse was close to death. A veterinary officer brought in from a nearby artillery unit had seen this kind of contorted pain in a horse before and said that is was likely Warrior had swallowed a nail, probably with his hay, and that if it didn't kill him the nail would work its way through the intestine. Seely spoke to his Warrior in his own quiet way and for a moment his soothing words and hushed tone gave the horse some sense of calm, but it didn't last. Warrior thrashed around, threw himself on the ground, kicking his legs in the air and crying out in pain. All Seely could do was trust in the vet's words and sit with Warrior until either the pain had passed or he witnessed the end. He watched over him all night and was well rewarded: after a tense few hours in which Warrior continued to writhe in pain and eventually collapsed, the vet was able to administer an injection that revived him. Warrior had survived yet another extraordinary ordeal.

Warrior

If Warrior had died that night it would have been the cruellest cut for Seely, who had already endured the news that Cinderella had passed away while he was in France. She had given birth to a foal and the children had named the funny, hairy-legged chap Isaac. The foal's lively nature seemed to fill her days and make her as happy as she had been when Warrior was home. But the little one had a passion for jumping, and one day he set his sights too high and he tumbled, breaking his neck. Cinderella was inconsolable. Without Isaac, without Warrior and without her master to lift her, she must have died of a broken heart.

Hard winter on the Somme

When the frost came, it crusted over the ocean of thick yellow mud that covered everywhere, everything and everyone. Horses were the only means of transport that stood any chance at all of getting supplies and artillery through to the front line, and that was hard enough when the ground they were walking on tried to consume them at every step. Warrior and his master often accompanied the sad lines of horses dragging their own weight as well as that of the ammunition loaded into panniers at their sides. They walked slowly, their heads bowed against the elements, and with measured steps, sometimes over wooden slatted mule tracks, which criss-crossed the mud flats. For the strings of horses tied together the walk was even more hazardous. One step off the tracks and they would not only risk their own early grave but take their fellow beasts of burden with them. Struggling didn't help and if they couldn't be reached and dragged out, they died where they fell.

28

Warrior

Warrior slipped into the mud several times, but being fit and young and without Seely's weight on his back he always managed to struggle free. There were a few lucky escapes, though, like the time he got stuck so fast in the mud that he became a sitting duck for an enemy plane. The pilot emptied an entire machine-gun belt in an attempt to hit Warrior, but not one bullet came close. He was also buried entirely, except for one forefoot, by falling earth from an explosion. He had completely disappeared, and yet Seely managed to dig him out unharmed.

Many horses lost their lives to the German fighter pilots. Observers would report the convoys of horses and wagons moving supplies and artillery to the front line and the planes would move in and machine gun the lot dead. The winter of 1916 was harsh in every way and the strain was visible on Warrior – his exhaustion was evident in his lowered head and slowed movements. Seely was aware of the effect the war was having on his horse and did his best to keep him safe and among friends. For both the General and his horse the company of the Canadian Cavalry was a comfort. Already a hero in the eyes of the men, Warrior was not just the General's horse; he was their friend, too. At Christmas that year Seely rode Warrior between all the regiments and batteries, and wherever the Canadians were a shout went up – 'Warrior! Warrior!' – before the men ran to welcome the horse. All ranks, from the corporals to the captains, crowded round to ask the horse if he was all right. If Warrior was all right then it followed that they all were, too. Like the men, Warrior was exhausted by the futile fighting, the biting cold, the unbearable hunger and the mud. But his spirit kept them focused on getting through, and whenever he survived the impossible they loved him all the more. They believed, after all, that 'The bullet hasn't been made that can hurt Warrior.' He was their lucky charm.

That Christmas Warrior was in good company. His closest wartime friend, Akbar – the Arab pony with the half-white and half-brown face – was still with the group, as was the sleek, black mare belonging to Seely's friend Antoine. In between the bursts of action, the horses would romp together and the men would organise races to lift the grimness. This is when Warrior was able to prove to the others that he was not just a war horse, but also a racer who could rip up the earth with his speed, just as he had at home. As the horses regained their fitness and strength they were all able to show off their pace, with Warrior racing to victory over Akbar along the beach – a little taste of normality in an otherwise crazy place.

The Battle of the Somme had struggled to reach an end. Warrior and his master marvelled at their survival in the face of such a relentless onslaught. In the heat of the battle Warrior had seen so many horses fall in action – he had lost several companions cut down by machine-gun fire and destroyed as shells rained down during a charge. As an officer's horse he had not suffered from starvation and cold, as some of the other horses had – he had never been so hungry that he had eaten his own blanket, and its buckle, too. But he had certainly known fears of his own and faced them, including the smell of blood.

'Warrior, we can't go home yet. I know you are tired – I am tired, our friends the Canadians are tired, too – but we still have work to do here and I need you to be strong a little longer for me. Can you do that, my Warrior?' Seely sat and shared his fears with his horse in a way that a General could never quite do with a person. He had just received orders requesting that he move back to the Somme battlefield in a covert mission to try and catch out the Germans who had returned there, and he was afraid of what he might find. The past few days had been a world away from the reality of war and now he had to ask his faithful Warrior to carry him once more, this time through the night, first battling the extreme cold and then the relentless rain, sleet and snow. Seely felt the warmth of Warrior's cheek on his own and thanked his glorious horse once more. He knew that no man could ask more of his horse, or more from his friend.

The Canadian Cavalry: 'Seely's Lions'

This was the moment in combat that Seely had promised his Canadian Cavalry, himself and Warrior, too. As the march took them back through Amiens, Seely received news that the Germans were retreating from the Somme. Due to march on the battlefield at 3 a.m. and frustrated that there was now no need, Seely not only had a change of fortune, he had a change of mind. He would not stand down the Cavalry. He knew what he was going to do. 'Warrior, we are not going back,' he said. 'Not this time. So many times of late we have had to pull back, but tonight we go forward.' Warrior lifted his beautiful, chiselled head to catch every word his master said. He snorted a little and shifted his forefeet as if he had read Seely's mind and knew they were going to take the villages of Equancourt and Guyencourt back from the Germans.

Galloping into Equancourt was a victory in more ways than one. It was only the third time the Allied cavalry had ridden to victory since October 1914.

When Seely and the Strathcona's regiment captured Equancourt it was a glorious success and a much-needed morale boost for the entire brigade, who happily rounded up German prisoners. Once more, Warrior was in his element and keen to get into the fray. So keen that it was difficult to hold him back from the gallop. Seely loved these moments when he could feel Warrior's body tense beneath him like a giant power pack.

Although a small number of men and horses were lost in that skirmish, the overall effect was that it inspired the Canadians – it renewed their belief in themselves and their purpose as cavalrymen. On 27 March 1917 came the blessing of a snowstorm. Visibility was dreadful and that was all Lieutenant Frederick Harvey needed to make his move. Only one problem: there was an old adversary in the way – machine guns. Harvey was cantering through the snow ahead of his troop of Strathcona's when the rattle of the guns began. The machine gun was in a trench dug into a slope in the walls of the village and ideally situated to pick off anyone entering the village. Harvey didn't want his men to be in danger, so, using the cover of the snow, he galloped them over to a ridge to shelter. Meanwhile, he intended to deal with the gun himself. All he needed to do was calculate how quickly the gunner could reload. A clip carried forty rounds, and when they were used up his plan had a slim chance of success.

Isabel George

The light was fading and the sleet was lashing down in sheets of grey when suddenly the gun fell silent. Within that split second Harvey turned his horse and galloped full pelt towards the gun position. A hundred yards before the wire barricade he took out his Colt revolver, still galloping for all he was worth, and pointed it at the enemy. His horse leapt clear over the wire and crashed down on the German gunner as Harvey somehow somersaulted out of the saddle and with a single shot relieved him of his duties forever. Taking control of the machine gun, the strapping Irish international rugby cap turned it on the remaining Germans in the trench. The machine gun post now belonged to the Strathcona's.

The intensity of the 20 seconds it took Harvey to complete his mission gave all three troops trapped in the shadow of the gun their chance to escape. Harvey's heroism earned him the Victoria Cross – on King George V's insistence. It was the first for the Canadian Cavalry but it would not be their last.

Seely, trapped with his troop, had watched the entire episode sitting astride his Warrior. There must have been a moment when he saw Harvey turn and gallop towards the gun and wondered what possessed the man. He probably wished he had thought of it himself. But the power of that one self-less act ran through the entire brigade. The men had been in the trenches for almost two years and were

34

spoiling for a charge and the chance to do the job they had joined up to do. The smell of victory must have been intoxicating. Seely's maverick tendencies probably rubbed off on his men, who must have realised that he was directing proceedings free-style and with all the gung-ho he could muster. If it had gone wrong and the two villages had not been retaken by the Allies, he would have been answerable, but Harvey and his fellow brave souls saved the day for everyone.

Once again, Warrior lived up to his reputation as 'the horse the Germans could not kill', and just as the men congratulated Lieutenant Harvey on his bravery (although he refused to see it as heroics), they gathered around to make sure that Warrior was all right. They must have noticed that his body was still flexing and flinching from the excitement of the adrenalin-soaked charge. They all wanted to make a fuss of him. They wanted to touch the horse that seemed to live a charmed life and brought them luck, too. They wanted to trace the line of the bright white star on his forehead. Surely a lucky star if ever there was one?

On 14 April Seely hosted a dinner to celebrate the Canadians' victories at Equancourt and Guyencourt, and to toast with champagne the bravery of his men and the award of the Victoria Cross to Lieutenant Harvey. Over the two days it took to take the villages, several of the men had distinguished themselves in the service of their country, and at the dinner Seely made reference to each one. During the dinner a telegram arrived for the General but it was put to one side, unopened, until after the celebrations were over. When everyone had gone he opened the envelope and read the saddest news: his eldest son, Frank, had been killed in action. Devastated, Seely called for his Warrior and the two rode through the night towards Arras, where Frank had been killed. The next morning, Seely wandered the battlefield in a desperate bid to find some trace of his boy.

The winter of 1917–18 was a cruel one, especially for the horses. The severe cold and hard rain made everything more difficult to bear, and Seely recognised that Warrior was nearing a state of complete exhaustion. The severity of the weather and the long and arduous march to join the Battle of Passchendaele was proving almost too much for this brave horse. Somehow, though, he managed to hold on, and because of this, others did too. The cry went out: 'If old Warrior can do it, we can!'

Laden with hand grenades and ammunition for the machine gunners they rode north towards Ypres. They hoped they had enough to keep them going, whatever it was they were due to face when they got there. It was a steady march in heavy rain that showed no mercy and no sign of lifting. The pools of water just lay on top of the ground until they were

trodden into the thick glue-like mud by the thousands of hooves and boots passing through. On and
on went the sombre trail of men and horses merging
into the khaki landscape. All perfectly camouflaged
against each other, their heads bowed under the
weight of the rain. Suddenly Warrior shied, almost
throwing Seely off his back. 'Warrior, what on earth
is wrong?' Seely asked him. He was concerned, but
also relieved that Warrior hadn't bolted, even though
he was trembling all over and resisting being
handled. Something was making him afraid of going
further. What could he see that was scaring him so
much? What could be terrifying a horse that had
stood fast as shells exploded at his feet and horses
were cut down at his side? There was a long line of
several hundred Chinese gravediggers working just
ahead. He did not want to go past them. The smell
of death to a horse's heightened sense of smell must
have been overpowering.

Advancing in the rain, Seely and his men walked
out of the gloom and into the ruins of Ypres. It had
been three years since Warrior had last been there,
and now they were passing by what was left of the
Cathedral and the Cloth Hall on their way to the
rendezvous point of St Julien. A northwest wind
battered the rain against Warrior's flanks and the
road blurred under the swell of so much water. It
was miserable to see all the horses lying dead along
the way. The mud had claimed them all when there

Isabel George

was no escaping its depth and grip. Suddenly
Warrior himself slipped deep into the mud. In
moments he was in up to his belly. It took Seely and
three others to grapple with Warrior and somehow
release him from the mud that was sucking him
down. Along with all the expected grit and determination, Seely also showed an incredible certainty and
faith: 'My Warrior cannot die …' he said to himself.
It was with the power of such belief that Warrior was
pulled from the clutches of death once more.

That was the end of Warrior's walking in the mud
at dusk. Seely and Antoine continued on foot. This
was no place for horses. Huge shell craters sat like
gaping wounds on the desolate landscape. Taking
only a stick each to help them stay upright, the two
men picked their way between these death pools that
were now filled with the merging grey of mud and
broken bodies. It took three hours for them to cover
the two miles to reach what remained of
Passchendaele and to find the remnants of the
battalion they had travelled so long and hard to
support.

The battalion Commander noticed the two men
approach and stepped out of the gloom to greet
them. As they shook hands, the few men who had
survived the last onslaught rose, like spectors, from
the mist behind him. The idea that Seely and
Antoine were there to recce a cavalry attack gave the
Commander the biggest laugh he'd had in a long

while. He assured Seely that there would be no galloping that day. Once again the cavalry was redundant.

The frustration of being denied another opportunity for a cavalry charge was felt throughout the Canadian Brigade. The truth was that the infantry weren't able to move in the mud, never mind the cavalry, and it was very clear why. The Battle of Passchendaele was hell for the horses and the mules. Ammunition and supplies had to get to the front line and the animals were the only means. Keeping to the mule tracks was vital, as a slip away from the walkway resulted in almost certain death by drowning. The gun carriages pulled by teams of four or six horses often just disappeared into the mud with the drivers still astride the lead horses. Men died frantically trying to remove the horses' traces and bridles so they could pull them free, but very often all they could do to help their faithful steeds was to hold their heads above the surface of the mud until they took their last breath.

It wasn't unusual for an officer to be called to shoot a horse if it was impossible to save it, and to help those who had never had to do this before the *Officer's Handbook* included a three-point instruction on shooting a horse humanely on the battlefield. The men were often glad their loyal companions could be put out of their misery. The close bond they formed with the horses in their care was something unique to the war. They shared the horrors of the cold, the lice, bullets, bombs and extreme hunger. They were brothers in arms, and Seely felt every bit of that about Warrior. He would often sleep beside his horse if there was no stabling, just to make sure he came to no harm. The Canadians knew this about their General and admired him for it. He was the General who always led his men from the front as they charged into battle, and the man who loved and respected his horse. He was a man after their own hearts.

As the mud of Passchendaele claimed its last victims, hundreds of thousands more horses were being shipped from Canada and the US to join the Allied war effort on the Western Front.

Warrior meets the tanks

General Jack Seely lived a charmed life in much the same way as his horse. Warrior had a habit of stepping out of very dangerous situations unscathed while others who galloped beside him were cut down in seconds. Seely, too, had a reputation for survival against the odds, and in that way the war horse and the soldier mirrored each other.

The General survived a horse falling on him and just about crushing every bone in his legs, but he recovered and returned to his Canadian Cavalry Brigade to rapturous applause. Every man turned out to welcome him back, and Warrior snorted and pawed the ground when he saw his master return. Seely described it as a 'homecoming'; after four years with the same cavalry regiments, the men and the General probably saw the brigade as their extended family. For the Canadians it was a matter of trust: their General always led them from the front on his brave horse, Warrior. He was not a General who commanded from a remote position miles from the action. So on his return, despite his lingering injuries, the men knew (if they ever doubted it) that Seely was prepared to die with them and for them.

The incredible band of brothers that made up 'C' Company Lord Strathcona's were once again in the saddle and this time they were going to be joined by tanks. Warrior had seen a tank before but that had been only one and it was not under his nose. This time things were going to be a little different. The secret plans for a tank attack on Cambrai had been shared with Seely some weeks before it was due to launch on 20 November 1917. The quarter-of-a-million-man operation was to be aided by the presence of an impressive 374 tanks. It was the first mass tank assault of the war and its purpose was to crush the much-feared Hindenburg Line into the mud. To charge through the 'Gap' created by the tanks mowing down the line, Field Marshall Haig assigned five divisions of cavalry – 27,500 men in all. The investment of men, horses and tanks was to secure, it was recorded, 'a most far-reaching effect, not only on the local situation but on the course of the war'. The 5th Division on the right flank was led by the Canadians, with Seely and Warrior right out front.

Cantering along the main street of Masnières behind a tank must have been a strange experience for Warrior. Being a thoroughbred, his capability for speed could have put him well ahead of the lumbering metal beast, so Seely must have needed all his strength to hold his horse back. At one point Warrior's nose was almost touching the tank's rear, and then – disaster hit. As the tank crossed the bridge over the Canal de l'Escaut the bridge collapsed and the tank landed in the icy water. Its overheated engine exploded on impact. Warrior had been on the tank's tail but had managed to sidestep the approach to the bridge just in time – miraculously, without a scratch.

The crippled tank sat in the water hissing and clunking and useless. Clearly the tanks were going nowhere, so now it was all up to the cavalry to take the initiative. A makeshift bridge had to be constructed to get 400 men and horses over to the other side. For some reason no one thought to see if there was another, stronger bridge nearby that they could use instead. If they had, no one would have started to build a bridge made of spare planks of timber at a narrow point by a lock gate, as there was indeed another bridge just 400 yards away. Ignorant of that fact, men and horses from Fort Garry's Horse were first over, and straight away the horses were slipping on the wood, which was no surprise as the farriers had adjusted their shoes for galloping on soft, muddy ground. Some slipped off the side and couldn't make it up and out due to the sloped canal banks; others were easily picked off by the German snipers as they tottered over the bridge.

Back at HQ, the situation had forced a decision to call the cavalry back. The problem was, no one could get through to tell most of the cavalry that. Blindly, the Canadians continued their part of the operation. When one squadron was faced with a line of unmanned enemy machine guns they decided to go ahead and take them. Charging downhill, swords outstretched, they ran clean through the chests of two enemy gunners who were just standing in their position in front of them. Revolvers came out to dispatch the gun carriage drivers as they tried to escape the surprise attack. Another squadron gave up the opportunity to take a group of surrendering Germans and their four machine guns and decided to charge through them instead. If the idea had been to fight bravely and leave the regiment's other two squadrons to gather the prisoners, it backfired. As the cavalry galloped on, the Germans changed their minds about surrendering and went back to manning their guns, hitting the Canadians from the rear. And as for the expected cavalry support, that was never going to arrive. The men and horses who had made it over the makeshift bridge before the order to pull back had hit troubles of their own and experienced almost total wipe-out. A trail of dead and dying men and horses was left in their wake. If Seely and Warrior had attempted the makeshift bridge and not received the order to retreat, they might have been among them.

Warrior had to be content with daily reconnaissance outings and Seely with minor attacks made on foot, but even they were risky in the streets and country-side around Masnières. German snipers were every-where. On the one occasion Seely chose another horse for one of his surveillance trips it was shot dead at close range and fell where it stood, with him in the saddle. If that horse had been Warrior it would have been the worst time for such a thing to happen. The horse was a military icon by now, a legend on the battlefield. Warrior dodged and defied death. Horse or not, his popularity elevated him to the status of war hero, and Seely was happy about this. If Warrior was a figure that could inspire men to fight for King and Country – and stay alive – so be it. But Warrior's popularity was linked closely with Seely's, especially for the Canadians.

In the wake of Cambrai there was much War Office talk about the role of the cavalry and, in some quarters, the political correctness of having Seely – who was every inch an Englishman – in charge of the Canadian Brigade. Cambrai could have showcased the effectiveness of the cavalry in modern warfare, but instead, due to the terrible consequences of the tank collapsing the bridge, it only displayed a cata-logue of disasters. The Canadians who served under

Seely loved their General – and they loved his horse even more. It was certain politicians who wanted the maverick man, the gung-ho General, to be put in his place.

What Seely and Warrior needed was another chance to prove the politicians wrong, and in March 1918 the opportunity arose.

The last crusade

On the morning of 27 March 1918 Warrior had yet another lucky escape. His stable, the dining room of a tiny French villa, came under fire and was completely destroyed by shelling – except for one corner of the building, which rather than collapsing into rubble had come to rest on Warrior's back. Seely organised an emergency digging party to get his horse out of the debris, but Warrior decided to do it his way and kicked his way out! Only the day before Warrior had been standing beside Colonel McDonald's horse as their masters discussed the Strathcona's, and the other horse had been shot dead. The two had been touching noses seconds before the bullet hit.

Warrior's miraculous survival gave him one last opportunity to go into battle. The Battle of Moreuil Wood was one of the last great cavalry charges of the First World War, and once again Seely and Warrior would lead the charge. In preparation for the advance, Seely camped under a wall and lay beside

Warrior, but their peace was soon shattered by a message from the divisional Commander updating the position of the Germans: the enemy had advanced further and captured the vital Moreuil Ridge, although the infantry were holding out despite great losses.

It was 9.30 a.m. on Saturday, 30 March 1918, and Warrior was waiting in the tiny French hamlet of Castel, just 10 miles out of Amiens. Four years of conflict had brought Warrior and Seely to this point. If the Allies were going to protect Amiens then they had to recapture Moreuil Ridge. Seely decided that his brigade had to succeed, so he gathered the colonels of the three regiments together to discuss tactics. It was agreed that, as the brigade advanced, Seely would lead the signal troop to the point of the Moreuil Wood, where a soldier, Corporal King, would plant a red pennant (with a 'C' in white at its centre) to establish the winning of the first phase of the battle and act as a marker and headquarters for the brigade. Everyone would see it as they passed the infantry line and recognise where they were.

Warrior, as if he had heard and understood his master's decision to charge, decided that it was time to get on with it. He circled and pawed the ground, snorting and complaining at being held back. It was sheer impatience that prompted him to kick up his hooves ready for the off, but Seely managed to restrain him while he took in the moment before all hell broke lose. He later wrote in his book *Warrior: The Amazing Story of a Real War Horse*: 'I knew that moment to be the supreme event of my life.'

Twenty men and horses had followed Seely to hear him issue the final orders for the advance. His advice was to gallop fast to increase the chance of success. Warrior was ready and rising to the charge. Seely later wrote: 'All sensation of fear had vanished from him as he galloped on at racing speed.'

The charge drew a hail of bullets from the enemy as Seely and his signal troop galloped on towards the point of the wood. Pockets of enemy fire thrust out at the Canadians who were at full stretch, with Corporal King making ready to jab the lance carrying the red flag into the ground. Warrior had free rein and instinctively began swerving from side to side in reaction to the swell of the guns. It was an inspired and thundering dash, especially for the rest of the 1,000 horses and men of the Canadian Cavalry Brigade who had the Hussars and the Lancers at full gallop behind them.

Warrior was still wrestling with his bit and spoiling for a fight as squadron after squadron thundered up the hill, the men's steel helmets in place to face the enemy. They covered six furlongs in seventy seconds, losing five of the signal troop along the way. The hillside shook as the charge moved towards Moreuil Wood, scattering the enemy in its path in 'paratrooper' fashion. Once it had begun there was no stopping the full force of the charge. The massive movement of horses and men streamed on, unaffected by the horses cut down by enemy fire or the men thrown from their saddles to meet their deaths. The rush of adrenalin transferred to the horse – nothing was going to stop Warrior from going on, galloping towards bullets and shells.

Communications were muddled and in short supply. Only the few gallopers who managed to dodge the gun fire made it back from Seely's initial charge to relay the extent of the damage being inflicted on the horses and men in the thick of the engagement. But no one had planned for the combined attack of machine and field guns. They opened fire and only a few men and horses escaped. The men who did were immediately plunged into close combat, with bayonets fixed against the enemy. The exchange was brutal and bloody and there was no turning back.

Warrior and Jack Seely rode through it all unscathed, as if they existed in their own charmed bubble. But it was not the same for the others, no matter how brave they were.

Captain Gordon Flowerdew, who had recently been promoted from lieutenant, won the Victoria Cross for the gallantry he displayed at Moreuil Wood, but like many of his countrymen he did not survive to accept it in person. Flowerdew was leading 'C' Squadron – a 75-strong unit of Strathcona's

Horse – round the northern tip of the Ridge. He had
already decided that he was not going to make the
mistake of taking the route the others had done
before him and leave his men exposed to gun fire.
He decided to go northeast to connect with a narrow
cutting that would give his men protection as they
approached their target. He asked bugler Reg
Longley to call the squadron together and suddenly
he found that Seely, on Warrior, had cantered up
alongside him.

The General reminded his new captain that it was
an important moment for all of them. As Seely's
grandson Brough Scott attests in his book *Galloper
Jack*, Flowerdew responded: 'I know it is a splendid
moment. I will try not to fail.'

The Strathcona's had seen enough that morning
to know that if they were to have any chance at all
they would need to go in hard. Swords drawn, they
prepared for the off, little knowing what lay in store
for them at the top of the slope. Flowerdew half
turned in his saddle to ask the boy trumpeter to
sound the charge, but as the lad lifted his trumpet
to his lips he was cheated of the chance to call the
charge. He was shot dead in the saddle. Flowerdew
shouted, 'It's a charge boys, it's a charge!' As the 75
horses rose up out of the mist, they faced not victory
but a six-gun artillery battery and the combined
rifle and machine-gun strength of five infantry
companies. The Germans had been expecting tanks.

The horses were cut down in just a few furious seconds.

It was basic and brutal. Faced with machine guns, the horses could not turn back or lie down. And challenging machine guns with bayonets had already proved futile many times over. Of the 75 men, 24 died on the battlefield and 15 more died later from their injuries. Flowerdew was caught in the open and badly wounded. Several of the men tried to rescue him from where he lay but they were immediately attacked by snipers – one was shot in the foot. Flowerdew was later carried to the clearing station for treatment, but it was too late. The brave man did not last the night.

An official war report by the Germans recorded: 'Moreuil Wood is hell.' And it was, especially for the horses. It was said that each man kept the last bullet in his pistol for himself, to avoid being taken prisoner, but many cavalry soldiers would keep the bullet for their horse to relieve it of pain and misery. The horses that managed to escape being mown down by enemy machine guns stood in the open ground in a state of shock and bewilderment, often dripping with their own or their rider's blood. Without mercy, they were targeted and finished off by German shells.

Warrior and Seely made it to the wood where the battle raged throughout a rainy afternoon and on until nightfall. The Germans had not advanced, which was a kind of victory for Seely and his cavalry, but the losses had been huge: a quarter of the men and half the horses (500) were dead. It was a strange time to have visitors, but the arrival of the French Prime Minister, Georges Clemenceau, accompanied by Winston Churchill, provided a surreal interlude.

Shells continued to burst overhead as the French premier surveyed the destruction. The lost and wounded from Seely's brigade wandered into view, and the wounded horses, too. Just a few hours before the visit, two soldiers were resting in the area with their horses when a shell dropped, killing one horse instantly and blowing a leg off the other. In blind panic, or maybe in search of a place of safety, the three-legged horse, named Spider, struggled down hill and found himself standing in front of the VIPs in a pool of blood. And still the shells fell all around.

'All my life had led to this'

The next morning was Easter Sunday and Seely invited the army chaplain to conduct a service to honour the dead and bring encouragement to the battle weary. He took Warrior with him to the barn that had become the new makeshift HQ and officer accommodation. The Germans had their own service on the hill to pray to God for victory.

Seely and his Canadians were counting their huge losses. The Cavalry Brigade was greatly depleted but they still had Warrior, their greatest symbol of endurance and hope. 'Here comes old Warrior!' the cry went out. The men crowded around him and stroked his neck and flanks in thankfulness that this horse, at least, had been spared death. As long as Warrior's luck never ran out then there was hope for everyone else.

Soon the terrible news arrived that the Germans had re-taken Moreuil Wood and gone as far as pushing north to take Rifle Wood (Bois de Hourges), too. This meant the enemy was now only seven miles from Amiens. The orders were that Rifle Wood needed to be taken, and this time the surviving troops would have to march there on foot. It was back to basics for the General and a blessing that Warrior did not have to go.

At 8.55 a.m. on 1 April 1918 Seely's men walked towards the German machine guns with devastating consequences. A group of Fort Garry's were hit by a shell, blowing the men to pieces. Seely was made to stay back at HQ, three-quarters of a mile away, but several times he had to leave the ruined barn to check on the men. On the one occasion he decided to go on horseback, the horse he rode was shot from under him. And as he walked back to HQ he was caught in a gas attack. It was a blessing on two counts that Warrior happened to be lame that day.

Rifle Wood was another slaughter and Seely was exhausted from the ordeal. He suffered after the gas attack, too. His men were fatigued, and out of all the horses on site two more had gone lame and three had been hit by a shell, so only a mule remained, which Seely rode back to HQ, slumped and coughing on its back. There was some good news: the position had been retained by the Allies, and Warrior had survived to tell another war-horse tale. Rifle Wood was considered a success (although at great cost), and it saved Seely's reputation with the Canadians. He was allowed to retain command and see them collect their honours; 20 medals were awarded to the Strathcona's alone, including the Victoria Cross to Captain Flowerdew.

Seely had his own idea on medals. He nominated Warrior for a VC and when asked why, he said: 'Because he went everywhere I did.' There was only one place they didn't go together and that was back to the Isle of Wight when the Armistice was declared. Warrior was left behind for a while to aid General Patterson through the period of demobbing and trying to return life to as near normal as possible for the French people.

There was plenty of emotion leaving Warrior behind, but Seely had been reassured that he would be back with the family for Christmas and he had faith in the arrangements. Few horses had such security. The majority of those that served in and survived the war were left in France for use on farms or, if past being useful, they were sold to the local butcher. Not the best ending to the life of a war hero. Others, like Warrior, made it home eventually thanks to their owners or sometimes the determination of the soldiers, who refused to see the horse that had been their companion for four years of war left to suffer a fate worse than death on the battlefield.

Warrior the conquering hero

On Christmas Day 1918 Warrior came home to the Isle of Wight. The Channel crossing had been rough but he hadn't complained. He left the complaining to others. The few horses that had made the journey home were all suffering from the same thing – they were terribly hungry. The cruel winter and impossible transport situation made food a rarity for man and horse.

The last time Warrior made the journey over the Channel, General Seely had been with him offering handfuls of corn every time the boat made an unsettling lurch. A handful of corn would have been very welcome and something Warrior had not tasted for a while. Weeks of meagre rations had reduced to almost nothing, and no one could do a thing about it. When Seely had sailed for home ahead of Warrior, his parting gift to his beloved war horse had been a biscuit. It was all he'd had with him, all he'd had to share with his starving horse. It was at that moment the man made a promise to the horse that he would never be hungry again.

When they docked at Southampton, Thomson, Warrior's groom from home, was there to take care of everything. He had one sole mission: to get Warrior home safe and sound for the General. The war horse knew he was in safe hands and nuzzled up to Thomson looking for anything he might have in his pockets. As the two of them disembarked they walked into a scene of chaos, just like Warrior and Seely had four years earlier when they had sailed to war together. And once again, feeling a friendly hand on his bridle, Warrior took the noise and confusion with placid acceptance. He had known Thomson since the day he was born and had always felt his protection. He knew that wherever they were going and however long it took, it was safe to relax – at last.

The untouched rolls and swells of the Mottistone Downs lay ahead, and just a mile away from his green and pleasant destination Warrior started to paw and stamp in anticipation. The fresh, clean air had worked its way through the mud and stench of the battlefield that had been clogging the horse's nostrils. Suddenly free of the smell of war, Warrior had the urge to gallop free. Thomson managed to speak to him softly enough and for long enough to reach Mottistone, where Seely was waiting patiently to see his Warrior again.

Warrior set a hoof on the grass and immediately looked down to see what he had trodden on. It must have seemed strange after the inches of all-enveloping mud and the pitted and stony roads that he had experienced in France. This was not punishment, this was kindness, and as he danced in the cold wet grass he bathed in its sweetness. He lifted his magnificent bay head and took in a deep snort of the crisp air and blew it right back out again. He turned sharply and there was Seely, standing, watching. 'My Warrior. You beautiful horse. You amazing friend and companion. You're home now, home where nothing can harm you again. It seems we kept our promise to protect each other, and now here we are.'

As Seely stepped closer to his horse, Warrior moved forwards to put his cheek against his master's. It was a moment they had shared before but not after such a heartfelt parting. Without wasting any more time, Seely took Warrior's reins and climbed on his back for a ride that took them the length and breadth of the Downs, galloping as if their lives depended on it.

Warrior's mother, Cinderella, had died while he was away at war but from the second he was released into the huge field around Sidling Paul he seemed to be looking for her. Over the days and weeks that followed he wandered the fields around Mottistone with one eye on something, and then he would run as if to catch it, only to find that it wasn't there any more. Perhaps he was expecting his mother to canter up to him and brush noses again or meet him as he slipped through the kissing gate, as had happened so many times before. But this time he stood alone in the shadow of the sprawling oak trees and just stared ahead.

Just as he had done when he was younger, and just as Cinderella used to do before him when she was Seely's charger, Warrior began to follow his master around like a dog, never letting the man out of his sight. Seely wanted everyone to meet his famous Warrior, and so the rest of the Seely family – his wife Evie, and their children – had to get used to entertaining more than the usual number of weekend visitors. Winston Churchill had been a frequent guest before the war, but this time he wanted a formal introduction to the now-legendary Warrior. During Cowes Week in 1934 Her Royal Highness Queen Mary enjoyed giving Warrior sugar lumps, which he took very gently from the royal hand.

Warrior was a celebrated war hero and Seely could not have been more proud of the horse he had bred and raised. Proud because he had survived all four years of the war, despite being in the thick of the action in all the major battles on the Western Front, from the Marne to Ypres, the Somme and Passchendaele, through to the horrors of Cambrai and finally experiencing a series of miraculous escapes during the recapture of Moreuil Wood in the final throes of the war in March 1918. He was proud for another reason, too: Warrior had inspired all members of the Canadian Cavalry Brigade, the Tommies in the trenches and the officers, too – and, of course, his master, General 'Galloper Jack' Seely. Even now, in retirement, everyone was coming up to say, 'Here comes old Warrior! Is Warrior all right?' just as they had when he'd led from the front in every battle they ever fought.

In July 1919 Warrior proudly turned out for the Victory Parade in Hyde Park and took his place beside his fellow war heroes, animal and human – much to Seely's joy. When they all met in Hyde Park, Warrior cantered over to see his friends the Canadians and rub noses with Casey, General Archie Macdonnell's horse. Macdonnell, Commander of Lord Strathcona's Horse, had taught Casey a range of tricks, such as lying down, playing dead and then jumping up when his master whispered 'The Kaiser' in his ear. Warrior had tried to mimic all of this when they'd first met in 1915, but in the year they spent together he never mastered the moves. None of that mattered that day in Hyde Park, though, as the two horses saw each other again and spent some time snorting and whinnying in conversation.

As soon as Seely's Canadians saw the old war horse they shouted out, 'Here's old Warrior!' and the men crowded around him, patting him on the shoulder and making a fuss of him. Warrior marched proudly through the streets of London, his head held high, where he received loud applause from the crowds. Warrior looked every inch a cavalry horse, and Seely had battled long and hard, particularly towards the end of the war, to prove the value of the cavalry – the paratroopers of their day, sweeping and driving the enemy from their position. Despite what his detractors said, there was Warrior: a horse who had survived it all and inspired thousands to fight with all their might for King and Country.

Seely and Warrior shared a charmed and heroic life that gave everyone around them hope. It was also a life of coincidences. On 30 March, four years after Warrior had fought and survived the Battle of Moreuil Wood, he won the Isle of Wight point-to-point. The same race his father, Straybit, had won in 1909. If it hadn't been for the war it's possible that Warrior would have been trained as a racehorse not a charger, but maybe the years on the battlefield had stolen a little of his youthful confidence, or maybe it was something to do with Seely's secret 'whistles' that encouraged Warrior to run faster, but it took a great deal of whispering in his ear and plenty of gentle words of persuasion to secure a pounding victory with his old trainer in the saddle.

A picture paints ...

Warrior and Jack Seely first met war artist A. J. Munnings (later Sir Alfred Munnings) in February 1918. Warrior was already a legend of the Western Front and Munnings, sent by the Canadian authorities to record the Canadian Cavalry in action, was captivated by the General and his inspirational horse.

The artist could not have arrived at a better time for Seely, whose position at the head of the Canadian Cavalry Brigade was being questioned by the War Office. They wanted a Canadian in charge, and although the Cavalry adored their General and his horse, the argument had gone beyond the men. Munnings's desire to focus on Seely and Warrior was ideal and the result of his work was astonishing. No one could deny that General Jack Seely and Warrior were every inch the heroic pair, and Munnings's portrayal of man and horse captured the essence of that heroism to perfection. His studies of the Canadian Cavalry on the march and in battle were stunningly real.

Isabel George

The friendship between Munnings and Seely extended into peacetime. Out of admiration and respect for the General, Sir Alfred travelled to Mottistone in 1934 to paint Warrior at home, a world away from the battlefields of Flanders. His collection of drawings encapsulated the relationship between the old soldier and his war horse perfectly. Four years later they celebrated their combined age of 100 years – the man being 70 years old, and the horse 30 – and still they rode every day on the Mottistone Downs, sweeping up and over the hills and dipping down to the water's edge.

Warrior died just shy of his thirty-third birthday. What a life he had experienced, and what love and appreciation he had received from everyone around him, especially his master. As a war horse he had put his life on the line for King and Country, and cheated death by shelling and drowning in battlefield mud on at least two occasions. He had dodged the bullet many more times than that. Warrior was a war hero, fair and square, but even heroes are forced to make sacrifices.

Jack Seely, by now Lord Mottistone and Lord Lieutenant of Hampshire, was feeling under pressure to rethink the corn ration he was feeding his beloved horse. Even before they left France in the winter of 1918 Seely had promised the starving Warrior that he would never be hungry again. It was a promise he had kept without question. But in 1941 the corn situation in Britain was so grim and Seely was so bound by his duties that he took the decision to end Warrior's life, but with one stipulation: it was to happen when he was not there. He could not bear it any other way.

They took one last ride together over the Downs, going to all the places that Warrior had known from birth and then galloping on and on, not resting until every inch of the estate had been covered, right down to the sea. 'My Warrior, you have meant the world to me. You have kept me safe when our world was being blown apart and you have been the best of friends in the presence of extreme hostility. Thank you, my Warrior. There will never be another like you,' Seely told him.

In the years that followed and before his own death in 1947, the General thought long and hard about the qualities that made Warrior such an extraordinary horse. He put a great deal down to the horse never being beaten or chastised by a human in any way. All he had known was love and affection from the people around him from the day he was born, and that is what he gave back. Seely recollected that whenever the horse saw the general's wife Evie, there would always be a display of touching affection. He would put his nose against her cheek and close his eyes. And when he was with the children it was the same story from the gentle Warrior.

Isabel George

On 5 April 1941, Warrior's obituary appeared in *The Times*. Penned by Seely and headed 'My Horse Warrior', the words befitted the honouring of a war hero, a loyal companion, a best friend and a 'faithful and fearless soul'. It could only have been written by one man about one horse. Together they personified honour, integrity and devotion to duty, for King and Country – until their last breath.

Harper True.
Time to be inspired

Write for us

Do you have a true life story of your own?

Whether you think it will inspire us, move us, make us laugh or make us cry, we want to hear from you.

To find out more, visit

www.harpertrue.com or send your ideas to harpertrue@harpercollins.co.uk and soon you could be a published author.